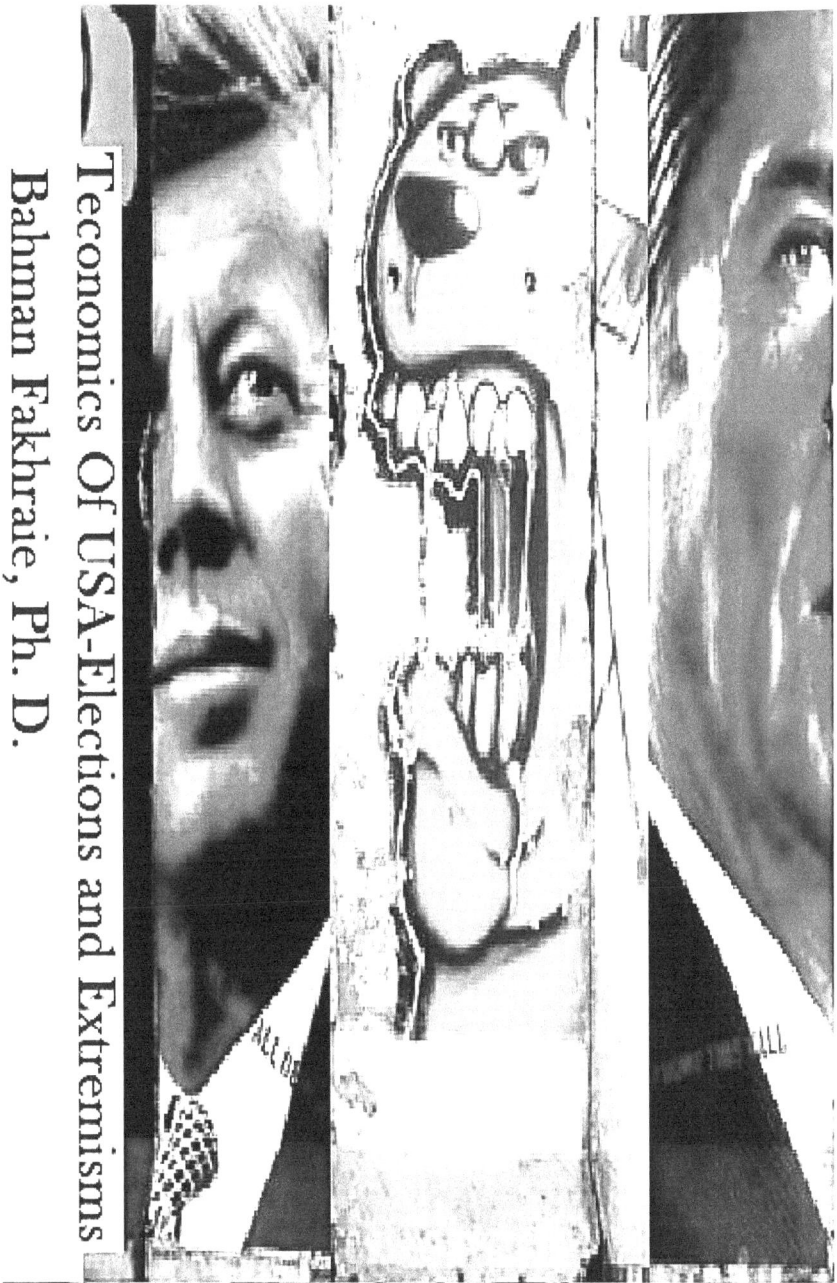

Teconomics Of USA-Elections and Extremisms

Bahman Fakhraie, Ph. D.

FERDAT PUBLISHING

𝔗economics
𝔒f
𝔘𝔖𝔄-𝔈lections and 𝔈xtremisms

By

Bahman Fakhraie, PHD, © 2015

$19.99

ISBN 978-0-9852958-0-6

51999>

9 780985 295806

DEDICATION

This book is dedicated to my immediate family with love, and all good wishes. I am grateful to my family Kay Davis Fakhraie, Lara Fatemeh Fakhraie and Anayat Wayne Fakhraie. They were great help in my recovery. I also appreciate my extended family in Dezful Iran, in addition, many thanks to all helpful friends here in United States. To all hospitable and free people that are so sprinkled frugally among humanity, globally. They deserve to live with freedom, prosperity, and in peace. I wish them, my family members everywhere, my readers, and everyone else and their families, Peace, good health, prosperity, and much more than they deserve. All good people deserve good lives with their families unencumbered by bad politics of greed, and technological tools of war and hate.

ABSTRACT

All political organization and economic system attract forces that may prove to be recursive to their productive models, or their constructive results. Those organizations that cultivate the freest form of inclusions are often targeted as easy pray for mischief or easy financial and political gains. The most lucrative prize of few decades past was the American colonies around 1700s. Therefore, the American settlers had to devise the domestic governments' functionality around protection of the governed, and later devised the union for further protection against the onslaught of enemies. The declaration of the independence (7/4/1776) and the constitution of the United States of America (7/10/1787) were devised to settle dynamic changes and arguments most unseen. Thus, their systems require informed and involved citizenry. Therefore, the injections of human and physical capital and technological knowhow became essential to their sustainability. Teconomics of USA Elections and Extremisms studies modern extremisms for their implications and intentions toward democracies, even, when they self-claim the mantle of protectorates falsely.

CONTENT

Congress shall make no law respecting an establishment of religion, or prohibiting the free exercise thereof; or abridging the freedom of speech, or of the press; or the right of peaceably to assemble, and to petition the government for a redress of grievances.

Amendment One, of the first ten amendments constitute the Bill of Rights in the constitution of United States of America introducing temperance, prudence, checks and balances in and on the new governances unlike the totalitarianism they left behind. It is an unwise betrayal of two hundreds and forty years of those good senses and governmental experimentalisms to abandon those principles for greed, fundamentalisms, and misguided odious theologicum that perpetuate xenophobic and prejudicial discontent and unsustainable malfeasants. All hard-earned principles were fought and obtained, and have to be maintained by the blood and toiles of the free and the braves, or at least your elections votes.

CHAPTER 1

POLITICIZED EXTREMISMS

Nothing is more certain than the indispensable necessity of government, and it is equally undeniable, that whenever and however it is instituted, the people must cede to it some of their natural rights, in order to vest it with requisite powers. It is well worthy of consideration therefore, whether it would conduce more to the interest of the people of America that they should, to all general purposes, be one nation, under one federal government, or that they should divide themselves into separate confederacies, and give to the head of each the same kind of powers which they are advised to place in one national government.

The Federalists, No II. Independent journal, (Jay.), Publius, G.P.Putnam's sons, 1888, p.8

We are into the fourth millenniums, the 1700s, 1800s, 1900s, and 2000s, that the constitution of Untied States of America has stood the American people on firmer political terra firma. All the while shifting sands, avarice, and time has vanished golden palace-mirages elsewhere. Nevertheless; recently, even the constitution is not safe from the bombastic bloviating onslaughts, and the supremacists Machiavellianism, and the prevarication and the exclusionism. Immigration has been a source of capital formation and job-creation reserve and a safe counter balance to the extremists national and international miss management of American resources from the inception. Even President Ronald Reagan fought the overt xenophobia, but you cannot keep bad ideas down among the expansive ignorance, and the bloviating ignoramuses. All good people can do to purse those words and compare and contrast them with the good of the constitution and the founding fathers treasure coves of wisdom, aged as they may be. The xenophobic bigots, the hate crowds, and the rightists' hate groups (not always exclusively) have seen it as gateway passage to the takeover of the three branches of USA government under different guises. The Political-Cooperate Postmodern-Capitalism, Wealth concentrations Schema crowds, and the Wars elitists with civil components of the unconstitutionally instructive militarism are pushing agendas as solutions now. However, those are not solutions. They are means of upwards redistribution, and interruption of checks, balances, and sustainable economic growth in jobs, salaries, and income of the Middle Class America. No economic sustainable solutions; idiocy, insults, land and Class Warfare, and global injuries are their failed mantra, political spin, and failed systems. The neo-fascism, NECON, Supremacists' Machiavellianism, and Neo-Zionists are working the dimwitted globally manipulated younger politicians into new failing war frenzies, victimization, and self-victimizations failing-war strategies anew. Nevertheless, the major financial beneficiaries of these patriotic war dogging are the war profiteers, few CEOs, and top one percent wealthy corporate capitalists, but everyone else pays the war costs, in human lives, displaced populations, and lost treasures. Americans' democracy and the Modern Pizza-oven war criminal ignoramuses are at odds, for good logical reasons! Logic should triumph. Nevertheless, it has been shattered by political spin-lies, and dishonesties, since the first year of Iraq invasion. Ultimately, the Americans, the people pay the bill for all the catastrophes natural and manufactured, as we have surmised for the last three decades, and two millenniums.

NEHELESITIC HATE-PROVOVTEURS INTERNATIONAL

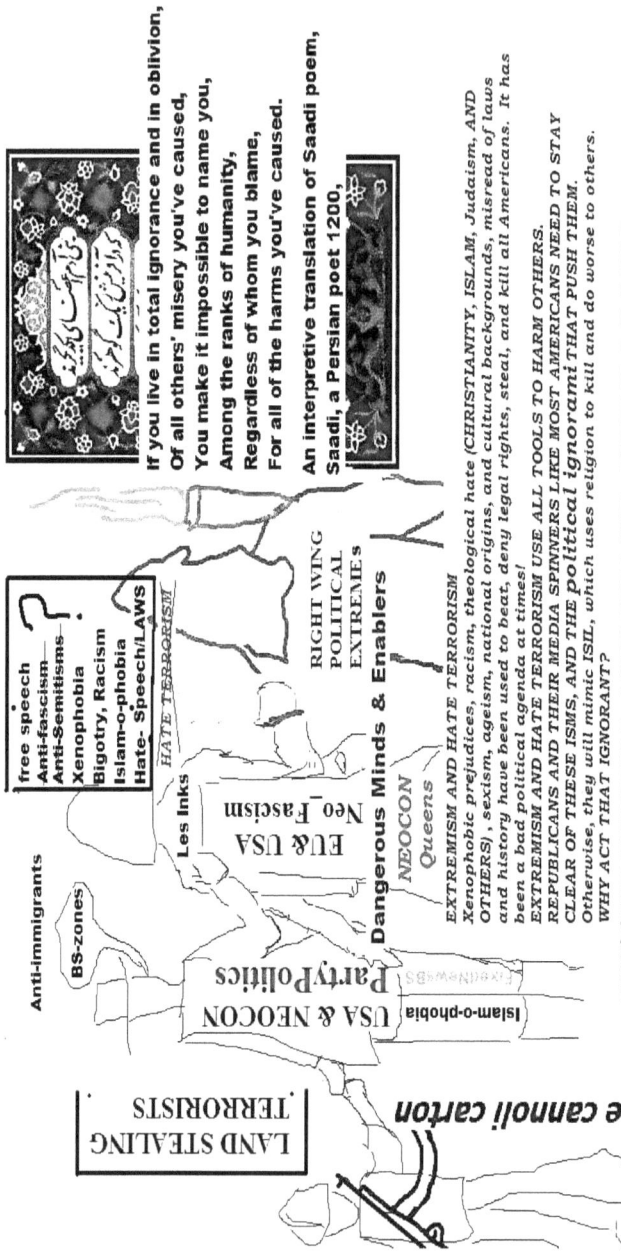

If you live in total ignorance and in oblivion,
Of all others' misery you've caused,
You make it impossible to name you,
Among the ranks of humanity,
Regardless of whom you blame,
For all of the harms you've caused.

An interpretive translation of Saadi poem,
Saadi, a Persian poet 1200,

free speech
Anti-fascism
Anti-Semitisms
Xenophobia
Bigotry, Racism
Islam-o-phobia
Hate- Speech/LAWS

HATE TERRORISM

RIGHT WING POLITICAL EXTREMEs

Dangerous Minds & Enablers

NEOCON Queens

EU& USA Neo_Fascism

Les Inks

Anti-immigrants

BS-zones

USA & NEOCON PartyPolitics

Islam-o-phobia

FixedNews®S

LAND STEALING TERRORISTS

The cannoli cartoon

EXTREMISM AND HATE TERRORISM
Xenophobic prejudices, racism, theological hate (CHRISTIANITY, ISLAM, Judaism, AND OTHERS), sexism, ageism, national origins, and cultural backgrounds, misread of laws and history have been used to beat, deny legal rights, steal, and kill all Americans. It has been a bad political agenda at times!
EXTREMISM AND HATE TERRORISM USE ALL TOOLS TO HARM OTHERS.
REPUBLICANS AND THEIR MEDIA SPINNERS LIKE MOST AMERICANS NEED TO STAY CLEAR OF THESE ISMS, AND THE political ignorami THAT PUSH THEM. Otherwise, they will mimic ISIL, which uses religion to kill and do worse to others. WHY ACT THAT IGNORANT?

EXTREMISM AND HATE-TERRORISM

BUT VIVA LA FREEDOM FOR A DAY ANYWAY.

CHAPTER 2

DEAL PEACE, NOT HATE

DEAL PEACE, NOT HATE & WARS

It is substantially true, that virtue or morality is a necessary spring of popular government. The rule, indeed, extends with more or less force to every species of free government. Who that is a sincere friend to it can look with indifference upon attempts to shake the foundation of the fabric?
Promote, then, as an object of primary importance, institutions for the general diffusion of knowledge. In proportion as the structure of a government gives force to public opinion, it is essential that the public opinion should be enlightened.

Excerpts from George Washington's farewell address, Philadelphia American Daily advertiser, 9/19/1796
U.S. Department of Homeland Security, U.S. Citizenship and Immigration Services, Office of Citizenship, The Citizen's Almanac, Washington, DC, 2014.

What most scholars wish, is that humanity will not inflict another Hiroshima or Nagasaki, Japan by modern conflicts, stubborn incursions, $50 million dollars lies-infomercials, and war-advertisements, and dishonest land grabs? It is assumed wrongly that it is another country, a third world nation, which will bear the full risk and financial burdens of nuclear conflicts. However, that may not be the only possibility since the post-Vietnam epoch. Insulting the UN, Americans, Iranians, and International negotiators, diplomats, scientists, and the Jewish pro peace voices are signaling that some republicans are sinking further in their extremism war malarkey and their persistent self-inflected economic funk and joblessness, faster than they can pick pocket Nevada to break into the white house. For which they will happily inculpate the immigrants, homeless wounded veterans, the middle class, elderly Americans, educators, workers, unions, and minorities readily and mercilessly. They have repeatedly attempted to fleece the social security laws, confiscated the Medicare and disability funds, and shut down governmental services for political propagandas. They will happily obfuscate and attack the Iranians, Americans, Israeli liberals, international trade, Peace, and Nuke Deals. The crass bear knuckle election politics are money-fueled with cooperate capitalism and foreign funding at the expense of all democracies, but especially the American jobless graduates, the Middle Class Americans, and the American economy.

The Failed Wars Eulogy Poem

From the ha ha land of enslaved COTTONs,
To the funny halls of wars' hos & hams;

Do not sell your good-senses cheaper to wrong
crowds,
To hate, fear, failed wars and misguided terrors;

The gentler wiser souls will come away, come
away,
From the rancid waters' edges, and those
ROTTENs;

You have run down the warpaths in wane, failed
and forgotten,
Now try your senses for peace, and the wiser up-
runs of WINNERS.
Bahman Fakhraie, PhD © 2015

The obverse republicanism once again fails with
pomp, circumstance, harsh self-defeating noises, too much
ventured, many fails, and nothing learned. Thus, separation
doctrine gets a church, military, and civil state revival, and
well endorsed resurrection. Once again, demonstrating to
the observant that in the political fields some logic wins

7

over no logic. Moral, ethical, good intentions win over self-defeating bad intentions. Something beats nothing. Center left and even Socialism, to the right side of confiscatory state-isms wins over self-enriching monopolistic corporatism, because self-enriching monopolistic corporatism as political movements behave like the confiscatory Marxism. Since monopolistic corporatism harms the middle class economy. Even if the Middle Classes are bribed with minor tax breaks for the middle class, they are under cut by usury-school loans, flat incomes, no-jobs and endless education loans that will defeat capital formation in the longer run. Fundamentally, and demonstrably the cooperate-capitalism has been a tool for upward redistribution of income and wealth in America for the last few decades. There is nothing benign about such cabals. Strategies that heal domestic economic and circular flow mechanisms win over the war only profiteering monopolistic-corporatism. Since, the war corporatism acts like monopolistic corporatism incarnate, and on steroids. Divide and conquer stratagem of past divided and lost votes in the past, and it will again in the future. Hence, the illegal and counterproductive anti voters' drives that corrupt institutional drives and fail the test of democratic principles, without garnishing collective trust or citizen votes in the future elections. Internationally, partners in cooperated efforts diminish in face of anti-Peace dishonesty and propaganda, and walk away for more trade. Knowing dishonest traders and exaggerating giants cannot deliver without cheating, when they are proven dishonest. One thing they cannot claim honestly, it is that they have not been educated, warned, or informed, about the clausal, catastrophic, and consequential down sides of their decisions, and harmful actions. Yet the good old Mississippi is waving down the old river, murkier than ever. American people need a working, functioning full democracy with at least, two independent domestic political parties, which will discard historic war-lies and blaze a true economic path forward domestically. The sustainable economic growth path required must have innovative job-creation ideas, with above the welfare-income wages.

CHAPTER 3
OBSTRUCTIONISM

The obstructionism and none functionality have been the result of their unproductive recent embryonic recoiled positions. Unfortunately, that makes many of them unfit to hold higher offices, or run for the higher offices they seek now. Their usual anti-science rhetorical bible thumping, their Koran burning crusaders' fears and warmongerings have escalated their uninformed hateful diatribes to self-destructive pitchfork politics for higher office. The political shenanigans in international affairs are rarely productive in politics, but they are very demeaning to friends and foes, they are good signs some rightists' political careers are at the fork in the road end games. Even after the colossal television campaigns' bills are paid. Some of these bills will have to be write-offs, in cases of personal bankruptcies among the usual suspects, or they have to be paid by those foreign funded foundations, and arrangement they have been made on those foreign frequent religious visits. Thus, Judeo-Christian ethic and charity moves and spins become genocidal war campaigns in or on another third world nation. The waves of refugees one after another should have alerted the media, or some alert

representatives from the targeted democracies.
Nevertheless, bills after bills United Nation resolutions are
discarded, until they are targeted too. Then the campaign
cash flow, and the media push spin their way. This will
make for another possible violation of election laws, or the
spirit of independence of the laws, as foreign funds have
found circulatory election inroads way past their tautology
of 'water edges' scenarios. Hey, it walks like a duck,
quacks like one, and really, it is a duck, not a political
party. We have seen and studied the source of the problem.
The attacks on democracies walk and quack like an ally,
but it has darker intentions. It is not to prompt peace and
tranquility, democracy, or even human coexistence, it is to
propagate another apartheid regime with extremists'
ideologies at taxpayers' costs, by the blood, and the
treasures of democracies.

CHAPTER 4

THE WATER EDGE

The bordering States, if any, will be those who, under the impulse of sudden irritation, and a quick sense of apparent interest or injury, will be most likely, by direct violence, to excite war with these nations ; and nothing can so effectually obviate that danger as a national government, whose wisdom and prudence will not be diminished by the passions which actuate the parties immediately interested.

The Federalists, No III. Independent journal, (Jay.), Publius, G.P.Putnam's sons, 1888, p.16

American voters and the pizza-oven ignoramuses of modern history are at odds for good reasons. Naturally, when total ignoramuses misrepresent and misread history for self-promotions, and intentional diabolic propaganda, often as paid services, the nefarious idiocies used to be tagged and bagged seriously at "the waters' edge." That degree of intellectual loyalty and patriotism rendered fake flag waving attacks, privacy law violations, and patronage patriotisms war mongering unrequired.

A new study of The Citizenship Clause reveals the first sentence of Section 1 in the Fourteenth Amendment to the United States Constitution. This clause represented

Congress's reversal of a portion of the Dred Scott v. Sandford decision, which had declared that African Americans were not, and could not become citizens of the United States or enjoy any of the privileges and immunities of citizenship, while toiling inside the United States of America. Recently the least informed often separatists, anti-federalists; and now xenophobic racists, sexists, ageists, bigots find unpatriotic means to undermine the union, the nation, and sustainability of the government by adding imaginary barriers to life and liberty of common Americans. Just take out African American and substitute any other nationality and legal immigrants, you will see the unreasonableness, and criminal intentions behind the bigotry and xenophobic intends.

*"All persons born or naturalized in the United States, and subject to the jurisdiction thereof, are citizens of the United States and of the State wherein they reside. **No state shall make or enforce any law which shall abridge the privileges of immunities of citizens of Untied States; nor shall any states deprive any person of life, liberty, or property, without due process of law; nor deny any person within its jurisdiction the equal protection of laws.**"*

Amendment XIV, of United States constitution, ratified July 9, 1868

How often we see and hear demagogues flaunting the constitution? How often the second and more important half of Amendment 14 of Bill of rights has

14

vanished in the media, or their perverse derogatory and demagogic arguments against immigrants, legal immigrants, and immigrants' citizens. Recently, how often we heard them angling to chisel a dishonest votes from easy bamboozled or uninformed citizens. Nevertheless, the insane crowds have obfuscated the water edge concept like the torture concept, like the constitution of Untied States principles repeatedly, as they have obfuscating USA constitutional rights and laws, and international human and civil rights and laws, intentionally and with malice aforethought. That was before they discovered Obama-hate mantra instead of political functionality, and the anti-immigrants' mantra, instead of domestic job and economic policy. They underfunded and gutted the education system (with anti-unions, anti-educators, anti-tenure and massive student loans' implosions and fiascoes), to be replaced by for-profit schools. These have excluded most minorities' urban areas, and decaying urban centers. They wrecked the American justice system, to be replaced by the for-profit-incarcerations-centers. These have disproportionally jailed minorities, and immigrant citizens on flex laws. When such bloviating idiocies run for political office in a democracy, the society needs to call them out, and hope that the population even with their limited knowledge will cast them aside, on the honey-hole of historical ignominy.

It is time to shut down the self-proclaimed oven-experts, since their productivity and political experiences do not exceed the realm of political entertainments. Statecraft and diplomacy are far more complex and less rewarding than these crowds could seek honestly, or serve ethically. There are no academic explanations for domestic barn kicking that those visits to Israel, or mystery foreign foundation funding, or the Nevada money will induce in the modern and seemingly honest conservative American politicians among others.

CHAPTER 5

HOLOCAUSTS

The entire Nazi experience and Jewish and none native Germans holocausts' history and industrial incarcerations included Muslims, Turks, gypsies, gays, and other victims. Those incarceration-camps were more extensive than the modern USA immigrant family holding camps. Christian white extremists, European supremacists' extremists (German natives with some American white industrialists' supporters, and other misguided neighbors and goose-steppers, and followers) orchestrated their slave labor camps, and medical experimentalists' labs, and oven death camps. All the while, other white Christians, all other races, and other religions, many Germans and others were fighting them covertly and overtly. The cabal is not too different than what modern day southern strategists, and white religious extremists of American south have concocted with the capitalists' corporatism on the American middle class, workers, students, faculties, professors, and educators' organizations, (whites or minorities), immigrants, and American Indians. Nevertheless, the severity is different, as modern day media exposures and ethical boundaries and backlashes are different. The Ovens have been replaced with joblessness, student loans, mass racial, poor, and immigrant family incarceration industries, and big bank mortgage-shenanigans, mass deportation centers and stratagems as unconstitutional inventions, and urban economic abandonments and decay, while the media capitalists abide them the appropriate coverage. Moreover, the rates of wealth extractions, thefts of the middle class and workers of their real per capita disposable incomes, and the transformation of the national wealth to the top one percent, and failing war fiascoes, grows louder or quieter for media attention span speed, and the conceal and conceit strategies that media moguls have devised. While the uses of ghost enemies for new-tortured scenarios often create fiascoes that victimize Americans, among other innocent people, and international refugees.

CHAPTER 6
NEOCONISM

It is beyond intellectual perversion of history but the ultimate act of genocidal dishonesty for the same white supremacists militarists' crowds known for their illegal dishonest theological and global wars to perpetuate more dishonesty, while beating their new war drums. Since they want to push a war on Iranian people for any ideas of self-defense that people of Iran can and will master immediately upon further sorties, attacks, and theft of their resources, in land and air wars against the people of Iran. The illegal and internationally criminal aggressions against Iranians are numerous and well documented, they are often manipulated and spined in ways somehow beneficial. The arming of old Iraqi military, (now the ISIS composites) with nerve gas was not a moral, ethical, or even legal act against humanity. It was a national and international illegal act. The killing of Kurdish villagers and Iranian soldiers by the induced aggressions and encouragements of the NEOCONS were also crimes against international laws. Hiding the foreign-USA election funding under new foundations or older Nevada routs with the blessing of new Israelis branch of the treasury or militarist' NEOCON inseams are nothing but dangerous betrayal of American election laws, and against modern true global democracies. While apologies were many, reparations are nonexistence, thefts of their Private Capitals are too often, and continuous, under UN banners, or other selective and bogus USA quick- domestic laws, or bogus tortured international laws. The fact that ISIS, DAESH, ISIL, Sunnis, and Lekud Jewish extremists, EU and global white supremacists among others are capitalizing on the factionalism strategies of the neophyte American politicians, only reaffirms the propositions into a more probable political hypothesis. First, peculiar political fights still have a USA water-edge marker. Those are violated. Second, the fake patriotism and foreign funding, their theological or cooperate legal masks do not pass logical scrutiny, or the smell test, or hide the political motives they newly conned into the inseams of American domestic politics. Third, failing foreign wars have prolonged negative externalities and societal costs. Four, none-litigated financial fiascoes continue. Five, they have not advanced homeland defense they have reduced it. The continual access and USA governmental inseams that the NECONs have managed in both political parties are a wonderment of modern policy shortcoming, and those massive security and intellectual failings. The takeovers of media, mass media, and multimedia globally only explain it partially. Neoconism and neo-Zionism have been bad for America and all allies. The dynamic Neoconism continuations have had clausal costs, and policy implications against national interests.

CHAPTER 7
SOLUTIONS NOT WARS

TWO-STATES SOLUTIONS NOT WARS

What has been happening to Palestinians (Christian, Muslim, and non-Muslims) are but small modern samples of criminal abuses of international norms, ethics, and international human rights, and media manipulations all at once. The two-state peace solutions should be advanced immediately. No new foreign conflicts, or terrorism dust-ups, should deceive or dissuade Americans from the real evil intend of the Neocons mischiefs. The facts that they have repeatedly had turned on American Administrations at time of war goes to criminality of their aims, and the Israeli-extremists paid-political intents. You have wasted your time reading this, if you do not think, they will readily do the same against Iranians, American people, and modern democracies, or any global democracies for their extremist-rightists and fanatical Israeli causes, beyond that abused language of absolute Israeli self-defense. We have seen the neo-fascism, NECON, Neo-Zionism at work for some time since WWII, but now we have seen them succeed against American interests for some three decades. The bifurcated insertions in American domestic political parties are structured by Israeli extremists' funding. They are creating and adding fuels to their NEOCON war caldron. Their hand and glove excursions are woven in NEOCON militarism, Treasury, and other offices that linger past one pro-peace administration, they have successfully tilted American two party system, and obfuscated the American constitutional democracy. The American constitution will also morph into the global war refugees of these prolonged aimless wars and warmongers, as political motives become blurrier past the water edge lines. The most vulnerable population, the poor, immigrants, middle class, elderly, and minorities are pushed under the baptismal-muddy-waters of the economy ceremoniously, and are kept under the water. Americans have become the victims of tortured political obstinacies of the anti-peace-land-grab agenda of NECON-lekud extremists. Overt pronouncements and money for political statements of the republican presidential hopefuls and other representatives inculpate them on their pronounced intends. Revoke this constitutional amendments, delete those civil rights, rewrite the peace deals, and march into the long-war agenda. There are no shades of gray with these new greedy fifth columns shameless self-promotions. The war on the 14th, 4th, 6th, 19th amendments are not hidden in emails, they are not confused in timeline and law enactments, they are pronounced on 24/7 news cycles. There is no need to cheat the timelines on emails, or murky the dates of new laws and accusations of illegal acts expo facto, all instruments the republicans have readily used to incriminate instead of exculpate public servants on duty and under attack. Those who equivocate to pervert justice and victimize the immigrants by subversions of the 14th amendment of the constitution, or by delectation the 4th, 5th and 6th, they will fill no duty to uphold the first or the second amendment either, regardless of what flowery language or New York spin doctoring they applying anew.

راهان پر پیچ وخم صلح

این سر رشتهٔ پر پیچ و خم صلح رفتن دراز دارند
هر گل و بلبل آنجشت بهاری بس باج دارند

گر حرف پنبه گل و بلبل پارس دست
هر کم دان جهانی بس هراز دارند

عقل کاردان قد دوست دنیا در این است
که در ساختن آن صلح منزل کاری بس هم راهی و هم داستان دارند

شعر دکتر سید بهمن فخرائی فروردین ۱۳۹۴

The Winding Rode of Pars' Peace Garden

The wishing Peace garden has a winding rode
      Every bird and flower of the Peace garden exacts a charge
If we band to weed the pars garden of peace en mass
      All the little minds of realm conjure all fears in dark
Wisdom are in the writing of worldly poets to ponder
      In building of pars Peace garden, there are many helping hands

Bahman Fakhraie, PhD, © April 15, 2015

25

CHAPTER 8
WARS FIASCOES

Honestly, whom are you going to believe? Their well-crafted lies, their fixed-media-spins will tell you another story. Alternatively, you can trust your own ears and eyes. In Benghazi, Libya, the ISIS-murdered American dead were not yet recovered, when PM Netanyahu peered up with a neophyte republican hopeful for frontal attacks on the American Administration, killing two unfortunate birds with the same dishonest stone. The blame games against the same American administration or American public servants have not dissipated, yet. The spiders' webs of entanglements, and the Israelis interagency Neocons, and their intrigues have expanded. The bloods of Parise-France victims of ISIS, DAESH, Sunni extremists were not dried. When PM Netanyahu showed to claim all Parisians' Jewish people for illegal land grabs promises in New Jerusalem. The land grabs continued regardless of Parisians, UN, or American human right lectures from prominent Jewish scholars' voices and others. A pattern repeated in the inflamed Middle East, where war victims' refuges are all denominations, Muslim, Shia, Sunni, and Christians, Jews, Bahia, and others. Jewish peace activists have known for some time the foundation funding's, Fixed News Media money, Nevada alligator cash pooch, New York investment fund reserves are their daily bread and butter aid money that have been rechanneled from American Middle Class, workers, educators, urban centers and their domestic economies into modern warfare, land grabs, and international failing conflicts relentlessly. The war caldrons of their makings are inhospitable for human habitation, wherever they create it. War mongering against Iran by southern strategist war dogs are only the newest bone in those old failing and dehumanizing dogfights. each time the dogs have new bones after a quick visits to the unholy doghouse, next to the holly lands. If the two or three decades of failing Iraq and afghan wars fiascoes teach any history lessons, it is that war profiteers do not end wars, they start new failing wars. Their success is in the continuation of American forever-failing wars. The dim-witted intellectual patterns have not changed from the Vietnam War to the present fiascos, the name of the countries, the blame games, people dead and dying, the waves of desperate refugees, and hordes of dispossessed human migrants have changed. This administration, American people, American jobs, and economy have also been the long-term victims of these failures, until the American voters have said 'NO' forcefully, and repeatedly, as they said to President Nixon's clever war crowds. Now they use the post war Vietnam's commercial slow success, as vindication, as the exculpatory proof of their 50 odd years of failing Vietnam War.

CHAPTER 9
NEO ZIONISM

The war on Iranian democracy of 1950 and displacement of that democracy for Oil corporations was by United States and the Republican Party manipulated by those multinationals. When the same criminal buffoonery revisits the United States population still in grips of joblessness, war depression, and multiple market crashes that the Iraq war and the same NEOCON incompetence have amassed on Americans, they hope for eternal acquiescence, ignorance, and patience. They have amassed billions in war profiteering, it is time for the Americans to send them home to Israel, and apply those billions dollars to repair the broken and divested American infrastructures, American student-loan-debt shackles fiascoes on Americas' future capital formations, and the chronic American joblessness, and the interrupted American economy. Which has been caused by the cooperate capitalism and the top wealthiest Americans; not the immigrants, minorities, the middle class, American educators, students or any union or worker groups, the governmental or private workers, or the elderly Americans. Most well educated American wealthy families already have sided against the cabal on their own. They and some cooperation have funded health and welfare, anti-malaria and for other disease controls, good water, and educational farm projects globally. The 30 year data accumulation and rates of decay in the real disposable income of the majority of Americans, the American workers, educators, the middle class, are not statistical anomalies, or falsehoods as the financier charlatans and criminals will assert repeatedly until America relent their economic wellbeing to the upper class wealth concentrators, media monopolists, and their corporate capitalists. The neo-fascism, NECON, Neo-Zionists are working the dimwitted globally manipulated younger republicans into new war frenzies. The bigger the TV-AD lies get the bigger the chances are for another failing war and more war funding, the more austerity will be pushed on American democracy, the less domestic economy will be funded. Under the piles of dead and injured humanity is the price tag of common land-war-toys. It grew from a few million to $5 and then $50 mils, while any coppersmith in any mud huts from south of Africa to north of Lebanon, to east of Afghanistan to end of Pakistan, to China and India can make the anti-war toys, the British land mines (the AUDs, etc.) for less than $50. The dollar amount explode skyward when the war machines take off to the skies. Nevertheless, the major financial beneficiaries of these patriotic war dogging are the war profiteers, few top one percent wealthy, and corporate capitalists, but everyone else pays the war costs, in human lives, broken bodies, and lost treasures. Will dishonest infomercials induce American parents to send their children to more dishonest wars, or kill more global village children with drones? Did Americans forget all the peachy promises of pre-Iraq war, Pre Libyan foray, pre-Syrian, or the older ones, the pre Lebanon promises? Those dishonest promises did not blossom in peace, prosperity, or American domestic securities. They worsen them. The war deficit did not buy more jobs for the American unemployed. It worsened it. The three trillion dollar Iraqi war fiasco did not gift Peace to the world, to homelands, or to foreign lands. It worsened them. The collective push to decapitate Libya did not produce another Island of stability. The unsustainable war-push foreign policies have added to costs and global masses of dislocated populations, and worsened national securities globally.

CHAPTER 10

IMMIGRAENTS, REFUGEES,

The free inhabitants of each of these states... shall be entitled to all privileges and immunities of free citizens in the several States...

Article IV, of The Articles of the confederation
BIBLICAL INJURY, REFUGEES, IMMIGRAENTS

The numbers of afflicted global populations grow with each precision bombing, droning, and the massive rise of the Terror groups. The size of the mass refugees granted dynamic processes some unpleasant that will unfolds in many years. The fleeting candle life-light of three-year-old young boy on cold beach breezed warm life in the empty shell of humanity, long abandoned by all occupants, leaders, demagogues, politician and commoners all. The perversions of familial units and lives of immigrants "legal immigrants" had been long legally harpooned even in economies that are more capable. The departure of decency, morality, ethic, or even basic humanity is nothing new to USA rightists' natters and nabobs that find sport in the legal disintegration of family units instead of the more traditional, ethical, and moral stand of family unity in all its legal forms, under felicitous flex immigration laws.

Nevertheless, it is all so important to see the global span of such inhumanity and its younger and older victims. It is sad that the injection of humanity is usually a fleeting second in the longevity of the long winter of our discontents, and the long-winded rightists' shameless and immoral propagandists, only at election times. In dealing with some issues diplomatically, and most economies locally, such human dislocation can be and should be mitigated at lower negative-externalities costs. It is often their last unhappy reluctant options to vacate their unhappy and unsafe homes. Why should any solid strategy delay much lower expenses, if not for corporate margins, and militarists' decision-making, instead of check and balances of the civilian diplomatic interventions? Most free thinkers already have their answers.

CHAPTER 11

ENLIGHTENMENT

POST MILLENNIAL ENLIGHTENMENT

Excerpts by Justice Robert Jackson majority opinion in
Minersville School District v. Gobitis,

*...The very purpose of a Bill of Rights was to withdraw
certain subjects from the vicissitudes of political
controversy, to place them beyond the reach of majorities
and officials and to establish them as legal principles to
be applied by the courts. One's right to life, liberty, and
property, to free speech, a free press, freedom of worship
and assembly, and other fundamental rights may not be
submitted to vote; they depend on the outcome of no
elections....*
*If there is any fixed star in our constitutional
constellation, it is that no official, high or petty, can
prescribe what shall be orthodox in politics, nationalism,
religion, or other*
*matters of opinion or force citizens to confess by word or
act their faith therein. If there are any circumstances
which permit an exception, they do not now occur to us....*

It has become too easy for merchants of hate, fear,
and loathing to attack all aspects of civil society from
airways, on multimedia, or on grounds in Mosques, Jewish
and other temples, to churches, and schoolyards, and
universities, from public squares to private sanctuaries,
from house of congress to the republican senate. Recently,

even the constitution is no longer safe from the bombastic bloviating bum-steads, and the supremacists Machiavellianism. Immigration has been a source of capital formation and job-creation reserve for national and international miss management of American resources. It is only recently, since President Ronal Reagan fought it, the xenophobic bigots, hate crowds, and the rightist hate groups have seen it as gateway to USA government takeover of the three branches. Guns, as much as lost sanity, adolescence alienations, multimedia megaphones are tools not psychopathologies, cause, effects, and human actions. All aspect of societal constructivism and educational forces need to be studied anew, they have never been deeply or holistically studied, followed, and supported dynamically, or repaired, as much as demagogues and profitable showmen have misapplied them for material profit and political gains. Illiterates and perverted electioneering are but new tools misapplied in such malfeasances, and denigrating politics of the moment. Unfortunately, short-term motives of the billionaire class, media monopolists, and financier oligopolies leave long-term harm in negative externalities and extreme unpaid costs, some of the mega billionaires' tax breaks need to be resented to pay for it. Those reductions of 80 to 50 percent Tax Rate to 35 percent cooperate tax rates and less tax rates have many provisions, all ignored for greed. Zero and negative tax rate are so far below the reasonable aspect of those assumptions that they are simply unbelievable. The repairers will have to start there. The ebb and flow of our emotional responses have been soulful but inadequate, while the problems of race, poverty, family, income gaps, health and educational shortfalls have reached less stable, and much younger and more adolescence portion of our populations. I am certain that condolences fall too short of the collective societal pains racked up over recent history of mass violence in United States, and even more globally. It is more certain that political leaders, and presidential hopeful that have invested time on true solutions rather than demagogic hate, sexism, ageism, and racism, and anti-immigrant agendas, have a better hopeful road map for the future of this great United States. Those leaders that have mapped out honest responses to these deeper gaps of inequities will find sincerer listeners among the voters and the citizens. Besides, they may have remedies to more of our current societal problems, beyond party politics, and self-promotional agendas for their own fame and fortunes. They may even gain rewarding inside in morality and ethical aspects of their public service. Their enlightenment is coming, whether they are prepared for it or not. Let us all hope we will do better in the new age of post-millennial enlightenment, so we can add to society and improve it. That is the Americans and globalists choices will always be the opposite of their hate agendas, if they choose unwisely.

CHAPTER 12
INCOME INADQUACY

INCOME FLOW INADQUACY

A 'Swift' Glare at the inadequate royalty compensations and real wage growth opens a holistic view of economic recurring weaknesses, and anemic jobless recoveries. It is timely and wonderful that Apple is 'Swift' on musical content, royalties, with their 30/70 royalty ratio compensations. Another quick helpful move 1/4 split for Apple could make them a Middle Class affordable stock holding as well, again. More digital-content Corporations like Amazon among other generous publishers can also make such adjustments in their corporate book and digital book content, royalty, and royalty distributions, and affordability of their shares. While other corporations are adjusting minimum wages and real incomes of their productive employees, the same employees that have been contributing to historically raising profit margins in the mist of economic hardship cycles. There have been trails of successful computer related businesses following Microsoft in amassing but concentrating substantial wealth among the very few, all-laudable entrepreneurial accomplishments, but short of helping the national product growth, and real income adjustments of the Middle Class, and student loan graduated system-victims. After all, workers, content creators, and graduates with decent salaries, and real incomes can donate to humanity after meeting their immediate expenditures, and student loans, with adequate and improved national income flows. It is important to understand the data from the next graph of growth rates in the American real gross national product over the longer periods (1947-2011). The late millennial and this millenniums' rates of growth and decay are telling, because of their unusual break with most of last millennium. It is neither irrelevant nor inconsistent to distinguish between major cultural shift from educational, financial, and economic inclusivity to retro sociopolitical and economic attempts of late 1990s, and early 2000. The policies are unfortunately are still in effects. These policies are a still pushed as solutions, rather than a wasteful attempt at exclusionism and counter cultural backlashes. As Author demonstrated in his book (Teconmic Analysis of cascading Millennial Economies, 01/05/2012), the population dynamic has shifted and will remain so for the rest of this millennium.

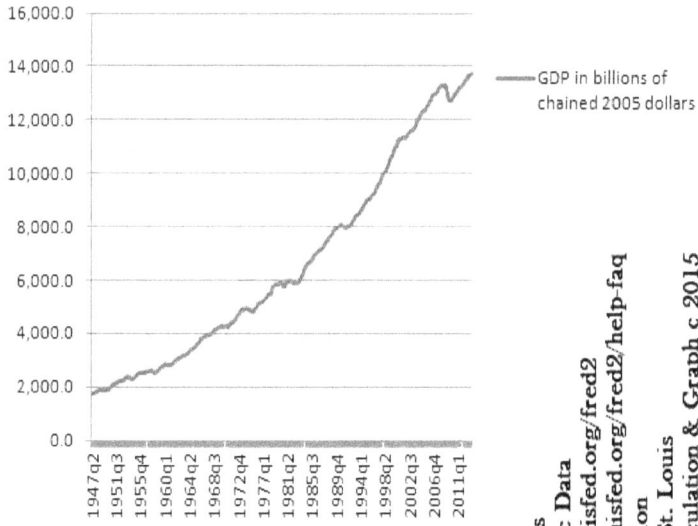

GDP in billions of chained 2005 dollars

— GDP in billions of chained 2005 dollars

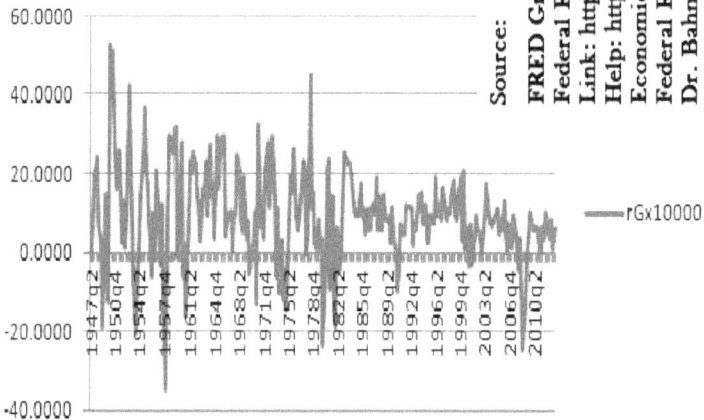

Growth rates index of GDP 2005 $x10000

— rGx10000

Source:

FRED Graph Observations
Federal Reserve Economic Data
Link: http://research.stlouisfed.org/fred2
Help: http://research.stlouisfed.org/fred2/help-faq
Economic Research Division
Federal Reserve Bank of St. Louis
Dr. Bahman Fakhraie calculation & Graph c 2015

The economy of United States of America can see a sustainable economic recovery unmatched in the history of such happy economic recoveries. That is why this is an important topical presentation. It will remain important in 2016 election cycles and political rhetoric. Nevertheless, it has become obvious to bean-counters international and decently educated economists that there are costs and negative externalities, and overt upward redistribution impacts that have left societal poverty, instabilities, and none sustainable economic conditions accumulated. The real disposable income stagnation and flat real incomes of the majority of Americans did not happened, because they did not amass educational loans and stayed uneducated. Slick billionaires, media manipulators, and their hired capable political fronts have structured a different vision of free-market monopoly economy unfavorable to the working, aging, and minority American Middle Class and their kids out of their share of real income growth, and national product. It is no small gestures that serious and hopeful presidential race leaders, those favored by the greater percentages of Americans are suggesting and articulating solutions for massive student-loans relief, and Middle Class income gap adjustments, and corrected redistributions and wage adjustments.

CHAPTER 13

DISHONEST BIASES

Brown v. board of education on May 17, 1954, Chief Justice
Earl Warren delivered the unanimous ruling of the Court,

...We come then to the question presented: Does segregation of
children in public schools solely on the basis of race, even
though the physical facilities and other "tangible" factors may
be equal, deprive the children of the minority group of equal
educational opportunities? We believe that it does.... To
separate them from others of similar age and qualifications
solely because of their race generates a feeling of inferiority as
to their status in the community that may affect their heart and
minds in a way unlikely ever to be undone....
We conclude that in the field of public education the doctrine
of "separate but equal" has no place. Separate educational
facilities are inherently unequal....

Common afflictions of bad habits practiced by the
ultra-wealthy ubiquitously and profitably are very difficult
to undo. Plagiarisms by billionaires and millionaires, even
as political speech, distinctly different from academic
research, are violation of current laws, especially now that
they have amassed historical profits, immense and
historically unmatched CEO pays. Which among the other
financial laws they establish, pass, take legal action, and
collect on others, but they do not reciprocate appropriately.
If one sees that traditional presidential campaigns of USA
democracy had been purchased away from the citizen

minority voters, but mostly the Middle Class Americans, for the last few economic cycles, they may be Correct. Now, what are we going to do about it? How and whom will the MEDIA help? Will the monopolies and oligopolies relent willingly to competitive forces of relatively free market economy, and the functional traditional capitalism? Will the money, or the citizens get their attention? The opulence class, or the Middle Class, the Opul-acracy and the upper half of Plutocracy, or the democracy, whom will they choose to service ethically! The three decades of data collations formulate the hypothesis less in favor of the Middle America real income growth. Screaming socialism, Jesus bashers, and global terrorists will not erase the immense harm that have been hipped on American Middle Class internally by the billionaire corporatists, and their employed political RIGHTISTS, far worse than the one off crazies and terrorists proportionally and statistically. All the while they have been pushing for funding small government, no minimum cooperate taxes, lowest cooperate taxation, and dangerous wealth concentration schemes. They have sucked up government revenues for their fleecing agendas. May be without the cooperate fleecing of the middle class, we will not need a bigger Uncle Sam job-agenda to dig out the USA economy from her chronic slumber for the ntimes. As it is, the economy will need higher minimum corporation tax adjustments, spending strategy, and budgeting adjustments, and higher incomes and more job-creations, which have been a point of contentions and irks the corporate tax welfare advocates. In that light, some hopeful politicians are humming Dixy walking in a darkening mausoleum. They have Americas' sincerest sympathy on their very difficult journey, but perhaps not the Americans' votes at the election time. Nevertheless, blocking and manipulating the voting rights, and pre-election voting, and minority voting are admissions of failure in this voting cycle. Alas, the fields of presidential hopefuls rightists are self-weeding faster than one can make pronouncements about the 1960's confederate flag, anti-civil rights backlashes, or the diminution of the constitutional amendments and laws back to pre-civil war and slavery arrangements. Will a magically sustainable economic recovery seal their failing faith? That is becoming a probable truism now.

CHAPTER 14
TWO-STATES SOLUTIONS

TWO-STATES SOLUTIONS

They have never had an idea for domestic economic sustainability, domestic USA jobs, or sufficient disposable income to sustain USA circular flow economy. Not even enough to pay for the wars, they have created or propagated. They are fighting American Health care law. They never even offered universal payer laws, or health-catastrophes laws to supplement it, or in its place. They are fighting against nuke-peace deals. They do not have a clue what to offer in its place, but more self-defeating forever-failing wars. Despite constant 24/7 financial channels, they never understood their only economic model of permanent wars, and the State funded dependencies on forever wars they seek, is a recursive dependency model. In reality, it is a tapeworm economic model, and not a free market economic model. If the host economy dies, the war financed economies die. If the consumers run out of real disposable income, the real flow dissipate, and the circular flow economy is interrupted, their tapeworm economic model dissipates, too. A jobs-based free market economy keeps the students learning applicable skills in schools for around six to eight thousand dollars per students. In the state and federal incarcerations centers they have devised arrangements that cost American economy upwards of 60 to 120 thousand dollars. The middle class wages are from 30 to 60 thousand dollars. The poverty level-incomes are at the mid-forty thousand dollars. Federal government subsidizes any income below the poverty level income as well. The same Private employers and capitalists' corporation have gamed that system for some time. Which political party or political actors have increased the jailhouses, filled up immigrant family incarcerations centers, and gutted educational funding as austerity plans. They have targeted the social security fund and Medicare social contract with the American people as flex laws. Alternatively, they have threatened to abolish them as give away charities. Which political groups have reduced their tax-rates from 80 percent to below 30 percent? The same political coalitions have managed to reduce cooperate tax rates to zero or negative. What party members have voiced breaking constitutional law violated civil right laws against immigrants and other minorities, while they have increased the social costs to these groups and the USA economy exponentially? Which political party has adopted such hate groups' agendas for party platform, against women, American Indians, blacks, legal immigrant Americans,

American college students, and the American middle class, and USA workers and educators? Which right-wingers have formally pronounced they will resend the United States Constitution on the first day of their dictatorial carination? Political Americans, voters, taxpayers, at some point should and will say no thanks. American voters would like our functioning two-party-democracy back.

HATE & STINKS

The cannoli cartoon

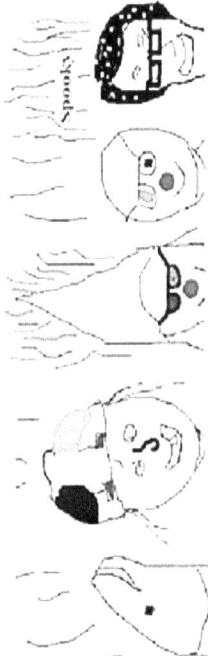

Spooks

Remember it for 2016 elections

They are against middle class, workers, working poor, immigrants' taxpayers, educators, and small businesses that make jobs. But, they are for cooperate tax cheats, and the 1- percent souls that horde cash and refuse to make jobs with living salaries. Go ahead give them billions and vote for them again.

Fixed Off News, Wacky Saucy Journalism, and Bombastic Bethlehem Bomber present the best new GOP politics that the American taxpayers AID money can purchase.
Mazoltuf dear voters and citizens

BIBIS-HATE BOMBS

THE BENEDIC ARNOLDS' GOP

EXTEREMISM AND HATE-TERRORISM

48

CHAPTER 15

CONSTRUCTIONISM

The Preamble to the Constitution of USA

We the People of the United States, in Order to form a more perfect Union, establish Justice, insure domestic Tranquility, provide for the common defence, promote the general Welfare, and secure the Blessings of Liberty to ourselves and our Posterity, do ordain and establish this Constitution for the United States of America.

Signed in the independence hall,
Philadelphia PA, 9/17/1787

Since we have come from better stocks of knowledge, it is time to shame the moronic clown-trains of incompetence, the xenophobic, racists, ageists, sexist, and misogynistic southern and global strategists, the political hate-groups' maleficence against all democracies and functioning economies into doing actual ethical peaceful constructive work of job-creation. American voters South, North, East, West, and global observers may wish for polite constructive political dialogues, but they have to be patient with these GOP career death-thrashings, until sanity returns, or, after the 2016 USA Presidential election! American people may earnestly hope for functioning reparatory economy, Jobs with their debt heavy private-college-student-loans or enough wages to pay them, or a functional true two party political system. They will not see it, with these rightists' political crowds. Just about the only way to turn the insults to injuries against all Americans and global good citizens will be to actually elect one of these pizza-oven experts, the TV do-nothing know-nothings, and the Israelis Fixed News Goose-steppers into the white house occupant, and higher offices. Modern democracies require at least two functioning political parties. Alas, one political party and one hate-group have not delivered. Senator Berry Goldwater nomination speech and consequential result should not be easily unlearned by the inexperienced hopefuls. Conservatives can choose better. Republican Party can and will self-construct. Americans can insist on it. They have done so for the extremism of the other party the Democratic Party, too. That like Peace will be good globally and good for America. Those who obstruct your voting-rights, or resend the constitution amendments are not on your sides. You do understand why they want to be in the Whitehouse. It is not to help you, the economy, or America. All votes matter, that is what 'we the people' means to deliver 'for the people and by the people', that is what the constitution, with checks and balances among the three branches of government can do, and has done for 240 years.

THE END

NOTES

*-The book front cover-picture is edited, montaged, and rearranged by author, form his pictures of The Wall Project paintings. Los Angeles muralist Kent Twitchell painted the portraits of Presidents John F. Kennedy, and Ronald Reagan. In addition, the Bimer's green bear is part of the ten sections of the Berlin wall that Wende Museum with the help local and international artists commemorated for the fall of Berlin wall. This is located along the Wilshire in Los Angeles, California, USA. For details, use the link, http://www.yelp.com.au/biz_photos/berlin-wall-project-los-angeles?select=9_rLCdr3E0h4calRUIkIXQ&reviewid=6A MXKYUU0WTctOa3Kg6yCQ

*- Speech Accepting the Republican Presidential Nomination, Barry Goldwater delivered 16 July 1964, iin San Francisco, http://apewiki.pbworks.com/w/file/fetch/70984420/Goldwa ter.pdf

*- A pain that will not wash away, a sorrow that lives as part of all parents hearts, Condolences, may GOD, ALLAH, and deities help all of our humanity to stand taller and our charity not to cheat us so frequently! http://www.dailymail.co.uk/news/article-3221090/PIERS-MORGAN-Don-t-shut-eyes-picture-did-make-right.html

*- http://www.spiegel.de/international/germany/germany-registers-sharp-increase-in-attacks-on-asylumseekers-a-1045207.html

*- http://www.nytimes.com/2015/09/04/world/europe/czech-republic-criticized-after-officers-mark-migrants-with-numbers.html?_r=2

*-From the time that the military knew what it was doing, in the short and longer run, http://www.huffingtonpost.com/entry/colin-powell-backs-obamas-iran-deal_55ec5acae4b002d5c0764339?ncid=fcbklnkushpmg00 000013&section=politics

*- And another EU political genius shows us the push, and the pull, and the clog that make EU holistic emigration dilemmas that have bedeviled American political rightist' idiocies, and their inroads into the hate political party systems, speech, and anti-immigration laws laws. http://america.aljazeera.com/articles/2015/9/3/hungary-prime-minister-says-muslims-not-welcome-amid-refugee-crisis.html?utm_content=nobylines&utm_campaign=ajam&utm_source=facebook&utm_medium=SocialFlow
*-http://www.nbcnews.com/storyline/iran-nuclear-talks/mike-huckabee-iran-deal-will-lead-israelis-door-oven-n398816
*- http://www.christianpost.com/news/msnbc-morning-joe-co-host-questions-mike-huckabees-christian-faith-says-baptist-pastors-comments-on-obamas-iran-deal-are-un-christian-142031/
*- http://wegoted.com/2015/08/carter-says-the-united-states-has-become-an-oligarchy/
*- http://www.cnn.com/2014/01/04/world/meast/lebanon-terror-suspect/index.html
Saudi Arrested In 1996 Bombing That Killed 19 Americans Lebanon: Detained Saudi terror suspect Al-Majed dies in custody, By Laura Smith-Spark and Mohammed Jamjoom, CNN
Updated 1:15 PM ET, Sun January 5, 2014
*-http://www.theguardian.com/world/julian-borger-global-security-blog/2015/jul/31/the-looming-august-battle-for-the-iran-nuclear-deal?CMP=share_btn_fb
*-
https://www.youtube.com/watch?v=vA7yz2vciGk&feature=youtu.be
*-http://america.aljazeera.com/articles/2015/7/31/west-bank-attack-puts-israels-settlement-policy-in-the-spotlight.html?utm_content=main&utm_campaign=ajam&utm_source=facebook&utm_medium=SocialFlow
*-http://wegoted.com/2015/08/carter-says-the-united-states-has-become-an-oligarchy/

*-http://time.com/3977782/iran-nuclear-deal-war-congress/
*-http://www.nytimes.com/2015/07/30/opinion/why-the-naysayers-are-wrong-about-the-iran-deal.html?smid=fb-nytimes&smtyp=cur&_r=0
*-USA government acknowledged the guilt, apologized gracefully a few decades later, and paid their fines for violations of human rights, and the interments of Japanese citizens in USA. The xenophobic, white supremacists' geniuses advocate ignorantly repeating the past mistake for others, but it will be terrific, huge, and kindhearted this time. The loud moth triumphalism emanates from the hate-America billionaires, not the greater-familial America, the middle class, minorities, Native Americans, or immigrant Americans. All of these flip-flaps and wars strategies are to hide their new no-job-plan for American domestic economy, and the redistribution of the American wealth to the top one percent. Regardless, how very good they are at political spin, the thinking majority of voters have a say, a vote. I am sure they are terrific with the ad-spins. They have effectively pushed the tax costs downward to middle class and working poor and tax benefits upward from the Middle class and workers to cooperate welfare kings and queens, by statist elitism along the way. Just how stupid they hope the great American people and voters are and how easy they hope it is to manipulate the greater American voters. If they let you vote America, You will have their answer!
http://www.theguardian.com/us-news/2015/aug/27/donald-trump-deport-11-million-migrants-is-that-even-possible
*-Two sets of people believe ISIS, DAESH, ISIL theology is Islam. One set is milking Islam for their gains in war booty and personal gains; the other sets are milking the hate for war profiting. They benefit from internal conflicts and factionalism they agitate among Muslims, and hate of Islam and islamophobia outside the religion, so caveat emptor. They are both, as far away from theological purity and

cleaner diplomacy as the driven snow in late winter
months.
http://www.nytimes.com/2015/08/14/world/middleeast/isis-
enshrines-a-theology-of-rape.html?_r=1
*-http://www.newyorker.com/magazine/2015/08/31/the-
fearful-and-the-frustrated
*-After 14th amendment, 6th, and 5th Amendments, we are
now deporting, dejecting, and rejecting the first
amendment. Will the anti-constitution Trump-ism be
triumphant by self-promotion and marketing? Will CNN
do better than FOX, and other media and journalists, after
the Trump-ism changes targets? Will The Middle Class,
women, and other minorities get better media coverage
than the immigrants? It is entertainment, while the ratings
hold up at our expense. So enjoy it. Nevertheless, can the
country afford the luxury, the victim-victimizations, the
birther bigotry, well, we will see. America has survived
worst demagogues and dog-vessel rightists' extremists, but
we will all pay a price for the joy rides! This will be no
different from the other ones. American has stayed greater
by parsing the malarkey, and not slurping it whole-hugs!
Americans have never chosen a hate-political party for
long, on their way to greater America. Never the less, if
you think a little harder and longer than your arousals last,
you will deduct the difference among noise. There are big
differences among the hate, loathing, and love of country in
the bloviating purchased sound bites.
http://www.newyorker.com/magazine/2015/08/31/the-
fearful-and-the-frustrated

REFERENCES

Books Links: Published Paperbacks/ from the prints & e-books lists:

*-The information presented in The Citizen's Almanac is considered public information and may be distributed or copied without alteration unless otherwise specified. The citation should be:

U.S. Department of Homeland Security, U.S. Citizenship and Immigration Services, Office of Citizenship, The Citizen's Almanac, Washington, DC, 2014.

US Government Printing Office

*-a- http://www.amazon.com/Dr.-Bahman-Fakhraie/e/B00IKAR1CM/ref=ntt_athr_dp_pel_1

b- http://bahfecon.wix.com/bahfecon

c- http://drbahfecon.wix.com/teconomics

*- Dr. Bahman Fakhraie, Teconomic Analysis of Cascading Millennial Economies,

https://www.createspace.com/4187823

*- Bahman Fakhraie, PhD., DEMAND AND SUPPLY SIDES OF TECHNOLOGICAL INJECTIONS,

*- Bahman Fakhraie, PhD., TECONOMICS, Utah

FERDAT Publishing 2012,

https://www.createspace.com/4196760

*-Dr. Bahman Fakhraie, Technological injection, dynamic new capital measurements, and Production Theory in Economics,

*- Dr. Bahman Fakhraie, POLITICAL MONOPOLISTIC CAPITALISM,

WEALTH CONCENTRATION SCHEMA, UNITED STATES TECONOMIC ANALYSIS, 2014, Utah, Ferdat Publishing, 2013,

https://www.createspace.com/4631870

*- Dr. Bahman Fakhraie, Teconomics of the Budget Ethics: Hidden Figures or Invisible Hands of Free market capitalism, Utah, Ferdat Publishing, 2014

*-Dr. Bahman Fakhraie, Technological injections, Dynamic new Capital Measurements, And Production Theory In Economics, Utah, Ferdat Publishing, 2014,

https://www.createspace.com/4740587

*- Dr. Bahman Fakhraie, Teconomics of the Budget Ethics: Hidden Figures or Invisible Hands of Free market capitalism, Utah, Ferdat Publishing, 2014,

*- Politeconomics: Political Teconomics

Paperback– Utah, Ferdat Publishing, December 8, 2014,

*- Teconomics Of Catastrophes:

All natural Disasters, Dynamic risks & Energy Resource Production Disasters, Utah, Ferdat Publishing, 2015,

Bahman Fakhraie, PhD © 2015

*- http://www.politico.com/blogs/media/2015/08/univision-chief-lambasts-trump-for-ramos-ouster-213028.html?ml=tl_11&cmpid=sf

*-http://www.nytimes.com/2015/08/16/technology/inside-amazon-wrestling-big-ideas-in-a-bruising-workplace.html?action=click&contentCollection=Technology&module=MostPopularFB&version=Full&region=Marginalia&src=me&pgtype=article

*-
http://www.nytimes.com/2015/08/18/technology/amazon-bezos-workplace-management-practices.html

*- http://www.msnbc.com/msnbc/donald-trump-told-quit-playing-neil-young-hit-campaign-song?cid=sm_fb_msnbc

*-
http://www.foxnews.com/entertainment/2015/06/22/swift-reversal-apple-changes-music-royalties-policy-after-taylor-complains/

-http://www.marketwatch.com/story/taylor-swift-withholds-1989-album-from-apple-music-2015-06-21?siteid=rss&rss=1

*- Two sets of people believe ISIS, DAESH, ISIL theology is Islam. One set is milking Islam for their gain war booty and personal gains; the other sets are milking the hate for war profiting. They are both as far away from theological purity as the driven snow.

http://www.nytimes.com/2015/08/14/world/middleeast/isis-enshrines-a-theology-of-rape.html?_r=1

Dr. Bahman Fakhraie (Author),

http://www.amazon.com/Analytical-Remedies-Millennial-Cascading-Economic/dp/0985295864/ref=la_B00IKAR1CM_1_2/190-0638945-5362843?s=books&ie=UTF8&qid=1434992104&sr=1-2

'Analytical Remedies For The Millennial Cascading Economic Declines: Teconomic Analysis of Modern Political Economic' – March 1, 2013

ISBN-13: 978-0985295868ISBN-10: 0985295864

*-

Dr. Bahman Fakhraie (Author),

http://www.amazon.com/Political-Monopolistic-Capitalism-Wealth-Concentration/dp/0989453995/ref=la_B00IKAR1CM_1_4/190-0638945-5362843?s=books&ie=UTF8&qid=1434992104&sr=1-4

'Political Monopolistic Capitalism, Wealth Concentration Schema: The Haves, The Have-Nothings, And The Have-Less; – January 21, 2014

FERDAT

FAKHRAIE EDUCATION RESEARCH
DEVELOPMENT AND TRUST

FERDT

FERDAT

*Fakhraie Education Research
Development And Trust*

Organization, Fakhraie Bahman

Grant proposal by

Bahman Fakhraie, PhD, ©, ®, ™

Budgetary, Managerial Directive and Legal Clauses

Legal letter and charges for unauthorized information use.

Legal letter is in cases of e-fraud, misuse of firms' information, or harm under sec. G. All linked and relaying entities, institutions, governmental agencies are accountable no exception.

Dear Sirs, persons, INC., (illegal use of firms' info), your current bill is **$10,000, ≤Ceiling $60 mils.** On behalf of Dr. Bahman Fakhraie, FERDAT, and the firm, family trusts.

These are the current charges related to illegal e-fraud and all harmful misuse of firms information, after the first time we asked you to terminate all contract and remove our name, firms' name etc. on this date.

1-Illegal use, the unapproved initial use of firm's name, contact name, duns #, any and all information supplied to USA government for the sole purpose of firm doing business with USA government, grant.gov, and NSF, Universities, other governmental and tribal entities, and all grantors. Minimum charges are $10,000.00, up to the ceiling of $ 60 million.

2-Use of firm contacts, names, address phone #, TIN/#s, and any information related to that.

Minimum charges are $10,000.00, up to the ceiling of $60 mils.

3- Continuation after repeated formal request to terminate illegal actions, sending junk e-mail, junk mail, forcing this firm to send back, by mail and certified mail. Legal costs related to that.

Minimum charges are $10,000.00 per each event, up to the ceiling of $60 mils.

4- Interference with firm soul business, time sensitive writing of government and private grants, at grant.gov, and NSF, universities, private foundations, NGOs and all grantors, with 4.5 million dollars floor. The Minimum charges are 4.5 million dollars, up to the ceiling of $60 mils.

4- Absolute or required non-disclosures by the firm or Dr. Fakhraie will require pre-paid plan with minimum flooring pay. Flex-legalism targeted at the firm, or Dr. B. Fakhraie will be due cause for nonpaid termination by the same, and harm-terms of Sec G of private contracts.

6- Punitive damages are up to 60 million dollars, if you do not stop, after the first notification.

Please make an effort to pay your bill. There will be additional charges added and sent to you for each time you try to contact the same entities, after the same dated termination notices.

Dr. BF, this is part of the legal notices under sec G, or formal termination notice dates.

Section 1, Mission Statement

To formulate optimum functionality in management teams, in order to make profitable and beneficial contributions, and create opportunity for merited advancements, **to advance research** in my fields of study. Utilizing rare combination of theory and empiricism, cultivated in multi-cultural inclusive settings in academic and private enterprises, I enhance the management in productivity and completion of productive projects, or suggest corrective recursive evaluation and total quality control improvements.

Experiences, among fields of International Trade, Managerial, and Production theories in Economics, Finance, Personal Finance management, and Businesses, which modern business and academic institutions find very expensive to employ and too costly not to employ. My extensive backgrounds help me advance research in my fields of study.

Section 2, Budgetary Clause

* All initial dedicated deposits (inflows) will be transferred to a FREDT, or FREDAT business account.
* No allotments or contracts activity will take place, until full transfer of funds has taken place per contracts. The cash-accounting method is used for tax purposes.

* Alteration to submit to requirements and regulations will fully transfer all risks, fees, and penalties, and legal responsibilities, to the source of the requirements.

* There will be a minimum product list, or writing, or proposal-output for further research, which will be presented and agreed to at the initial phases.
* This will be the only output legally required at the end of contract, or at the end of grant periods.
* There is a managerial flow chart enclosed to enhance comprehensions of cash flow, read after the legal notes section.

Section 3, Managerial Clause

* Dr. Bahman Fakhraie will act as agent, manger, and soul administrator, Executives director, Principle Investigator PI for FERDT, FERDAT, Fakhraie Bahman Organization, with full rights to take legal action and make final settlement on its accounts.
* Dr. Bahman Fakhraie will act as agent, manger, and soul administrator for Fakhraie Bahman Organization, with full right to take legal action on its accounts.
* A general electronic bookkeeping is followed, on periodical bases, as grants require it. Current standard is quarterly, post full disbursements of grant funding. (FRR is required quarterly)
* Details, information, managerial technologies are legally protected, and no such disclosure will be made of the Organization, administrator, assignees, or representatives of FERDT, FERDAT, or Fakhraie Bahman Organization. All copyright materials are marketable, or further developed by Mr. Fakhraie. All existing rights are reserved.
* All informal and formal requests can be made by mail, or email.

* There is forfeiture of all advances, in cases of mortality, health, or attempt at disbarment, legal action, harm, against soul administrator, Fakhraie Bahman Organization, with full right to take legal action on its accounts.
* Any and all such request will have to forward additional funding for legal representations and undue imposition of costs or harm, please read the legal note and sec. G. It will always apply.
* **Alteration to submit to requirements and regulations will fully transfer all risks, fees, and penalties, and legal responsibilities, to the source of the requirements.**

* The reviewers will have access to a portion of the progress.
* Full transparencies are practiced for authorized agents only, mostly through the internet, after proper signatures are obtained.
* All future development, educational development will have to be contracted, or signed out temporarily.
* All copyrights and proprietary rights are reserved, granted, accorded to Dr. Bahman Fakhraie, and his living trust.
* The final product in initial agreement will be shared with the grantors, after all the financial settlements have been met.

* PI, FERDAT; Dr. Fakhraie, Bahman
Dr. Bahman Fakhraie, PhD, UOU, UT,
  USA
* Position Classification, Executive level
  I,
* Salary exceeds Fed Cap for private
  contracts.
* NSF ID, 000586796, Organizational ID
  Code, P 269878425
* Private for Profit Business:
* DUNS Number D&B # ███89684,
* CAGE/NCAGE: ███S3, Congressional
  Districts, UT_001
* Sec G of private contract always applies
* For other institutional DUNS, etc.
  Please, check cover letter, or contact
  PI. Thanks
* PI Information(dated)

Section 4, Legal Clause, All Right Reserved & Other Legal Notes
All rights will revert back to author after 3 years, if limited rights are contracted.
E. Speech, Lecture Tours, and Research Papers & Follow Up:
All publications or Grant-products are commonly published on completion, USA Library of Congress, Trade Journals, Or Author's websites, etc.
Contact for individualized contracts
F. For Time Donation, And Charity Events: 1. 5% of Net contracts paid
2. Time By Appointments Only.3. Write Donations Checks to:
Fakhraie Trust fund / Bahman Fakhraie
G. Any and All Risks or Harms invokes these legal clauses. The Following legal clauses are base minimum, and will not limit all rights and legal protection, with uniform constitutional rights they are implied and accorded. Contractually all rights are implied and accorded. Please, read all the legal notes before using any materials.
G1. In Cases of misuse of these materials, plagiarisms, use to put at risk of harm, or to harm, (Legal, or Etc.) the firm, CEO, FERDT, president: Mr. Bahman Fakhraie, His family members, it will result in $60 million legal action per each event in United States Courts/ any Jurisdictions determined or set by author or a trust set up by Mr. Bahman Fakhraie. Also, use of creative ideas and intellectual properties for any commerce direct or indirect or by proxy, expansions of outlines, attempts to defraud, over charge, harm with illegal acts, misuse of private and confidential materials, information, and properties, letters, checks, e-mails, faxes, any and all communications, and any electronically stored materials and pictures, or false claims against the above entities will be an agreement with and subject to all elements of this contract, and as a user license, without nullifying further and ensuing legal actions or collections, or as directed by the same or authorities. All other contracts are one time contracts and s. t. this contract. Please, notify firm, Mr. Bahman Fakhraie, of all infractions, transactions, or transfer to individuals or to private or government entities in accord with current laws.
G2a. All Costs due to inquiries, related or required business licenses, legal paper works, and hours, all costs related to corrective or reparation publicity, bonding and insurances costs, stock related activities, all costs related to any harm (financial & legal) will be charges to the sources and inquirers, and none to the firm or Bahman Fakhraie, his family, or any and all of their related assets. All attempts to harm, engagements, cashing checks or accepting cash from the same entities is an agreement with all elements of this contract.

G2b. All copy rights associated with written works and further development of all works remains with the author Bahman Fakhraie or his trusts. All development rights are reserved by the same entities.

G3. Any and all unsolicited commercial phone calls, to Mr. Bahman Fakhraie and, his family will result to a minimum of $ 500 per call charged to the source, due and payable in the same month the call is made, all other elements of this contract also apply, all contracts remain subservient to this contract, all costs of collection and legal actions also are added to the bill payable by source and not Bahman Fakhraie and these entities.

G4.All Consultation and coaching involves risks due to market, business, political, etc. costs and damages related to all such risk are paid by individuals or business entities involved and none is implied or taken by Bahman Fakhraie, his family, or any related assets, under any and all conditions. These entities' court fees are $10,000; et minimum.

G5.Uncomfortable conditions, misapplications of any law to harm, harassment, odd-hour calls, etc will be due cause for termination of services without refund, and are actionable per this contract.

§§§§

All publications or Grant-products are published on completion, USA Library of Congress, Trade Journals, Or Author's websites, etc. All rights revert to author after 3 years, if limited rights are contracted.

E. Speech, Lecture Tours, Research Papers & Follow Up:
1.   Per Each Event-$ 350,000 +.
2.   with Foreign Travel-$ 3,000,000
3.   Book/Cash Advance floor Min; Net Royalties ~40%
4. Scripts: /Starting from.....................$ 300,000
5. Movie Script (120+Pages).................$ 3,000,000
6. Or Cash Advance Plus 2% of All Gross paid annually
7. Consultations Fee/Initial charge non-refunded $ 10,000, & ...10 %
8. Business limited ventures, partnerships, etc. .... ≥ 30%
9. Salary executive level I

F. For Time Donation, And Charity Events: 1. 5% of Net contracts paid 2. Time By Appointments Only.3. Write Donations Checks to Fakhraie Trust fund / Bahman Fakhraie. G. Any and All Risks or Harms invokes these legal clauses. The Following legal clauses are base minimum, and will not limit all rights and legal protection, with uniform constitutional rights they are implied and accorded. Contractually all rights are implied and accorded. Please, read all the legal notes before using any materials. G1. In Cases of misuse of these materials, plagiarisms, use to put at risk of harm, or to harm, (Legal, or Etc.) the firm, CEO: Mr. Bahman Fakhraie, His family members, will result in $60 million legal action per each event in United States Courts/Jurisdictions determine by author or a trust set up by Mr. Bahman Fakhraie. Also, use of creative ideas intellectual properties, expansions of outlines, attempts to defraud, over charge, harm with illegal acts, misuse of private and confidential materials and properties, letters, e-mails, faxes, any and all communications, and any electronically stored materials and pictures, or false claims against the above entities will be an agreement with all elements of this contract, and as a use license, without nullifying ensuing legal actions or collections, or as directed by the same or authorities. Please, notify firm, Mr. Bahman Fakhraie, of any and all infractions, transactions, or transfer to individuals or to private or government entities. G2a. All Costs due to inquiries, related or required business licenses, legal paper works and hours, all costs related to corrective or reparation publicity, bonding and insurances costs, stock related activities, all costs related to any harm (financial & legal) will be charges to the sources and inquirers, and none to the firm or Bahman Fakhraie, his family, or any and all of their related assets. All attempts to harm, engagements, cashing checks or accepting cash from the same entities is an agreement with all elements of this contract. G2b. All copy rights associated with written works and further development of all works remains with the author Bahman Fakhraie or his trusts. Any and all development rights are reserved by the same entities. G3. Any and all unsolicited commercial phone calls to Mr. Bahman Fakhraie, his family will result to a minimum of $ 500 per call charged to the source, due and payable in the same month the call is made, all other elements of this contract also apply, all contracts remain subservient to this contract, all costs of collection and legal actions also are added to the bill payable by source and not Bahman Fakhraie and these entities. G4.All Consultation and coaching involves risks due to market, business, political, etc. costs and damages related to all such risk are paid by individuals or business entities involved and none is implied or taken by Bahman Fakhraie, his family, or any related assets, under any and all conditions. These entities' court fees are $10,000; et minimum. G5.Uncomfortable conditions, misapplications of any law to harm, harassment, odd-hour calls, etc will be due cause for termination of services without refund, and are actionable per this contract.

§§§§

Letter of Agreement with FRDET and Fakhraie Bahman

I/We (Ms., Mrs., Mr.): ....

Business Name: ....

Social Security numbers: ....../....../............ ..../....../................

Tax ID Numbers: ....

Driver License Numbers:

....

Passport (Birth Certificate) Numbers:

....

Have read all the information supplied by Dr. Bahman Fakhraie, and /or FRDET (Trust, LLP). Agree to supply all correct financial and related information and select the following services by marking (X), or Letter a b c, Or Number 1 2 3, or write and specify. Agree to the power of attorney required to confirm or acquire financial and related information. Plus a check for $3000, for preliminary registrations, legal and financial inquiries, and licensing fees.

  1: ☐   2: ☐   3: ☐   4: ☐   5: ☐   6: ☐   7: ☐   8: ☐

Specify which kinds of the following accounts you will require:

Individual/Gov. ☐   Joints ☐   Joint with survival rights ☐   Trusts ☐

    Details: ....

Business types:

      Ltd Partnership (LLP, LLC) ☐   Soul Owner ☐

   Inc/Gov ☐   Firm ☐

    Details: ....

I/We agree to pay the fees and costs as they accrue, after 30 days a charge of %10 per annum is added to past due amounts until they are settled or paid in full. That at least 75% charges and expenses are paid no later than six month after initial reports or outlines are examined. That all travel lodgings and phone charges, legal research, and research hours, I/We request are fully paid. I/We have read and understand the nature of business, business cycles, market price fluctuation risks, currency fluctuation risks, social and political risks, natural and climatic risks, and all other risks herewith not itemized; therefore, I/we accept all financial losses, responsibilities, all punitive or compensatory damages that occur for all activities that are undertaken based on or claimed related to the report or reports, advise and etc., generated by Money Wise Firm, Bahman Fakhraie or all the entities named, agents, and associates. I/We understand in cases of any false, misleading, or withholding information the Money Wise Firm and all entities named above will not be held accountable, responsible, financially or otherwise, and will be refunded for any damages fully. I/We release all others associated with Money Wise Firm, and Bahman Fakhraie from financial losses, responsibilities, all compensatory and punitive charges concerning activities I/We undertake.

Sign (full name, titles, and address)

 Business (Name, Address; Agents' title):

Section 5, Organization Chart

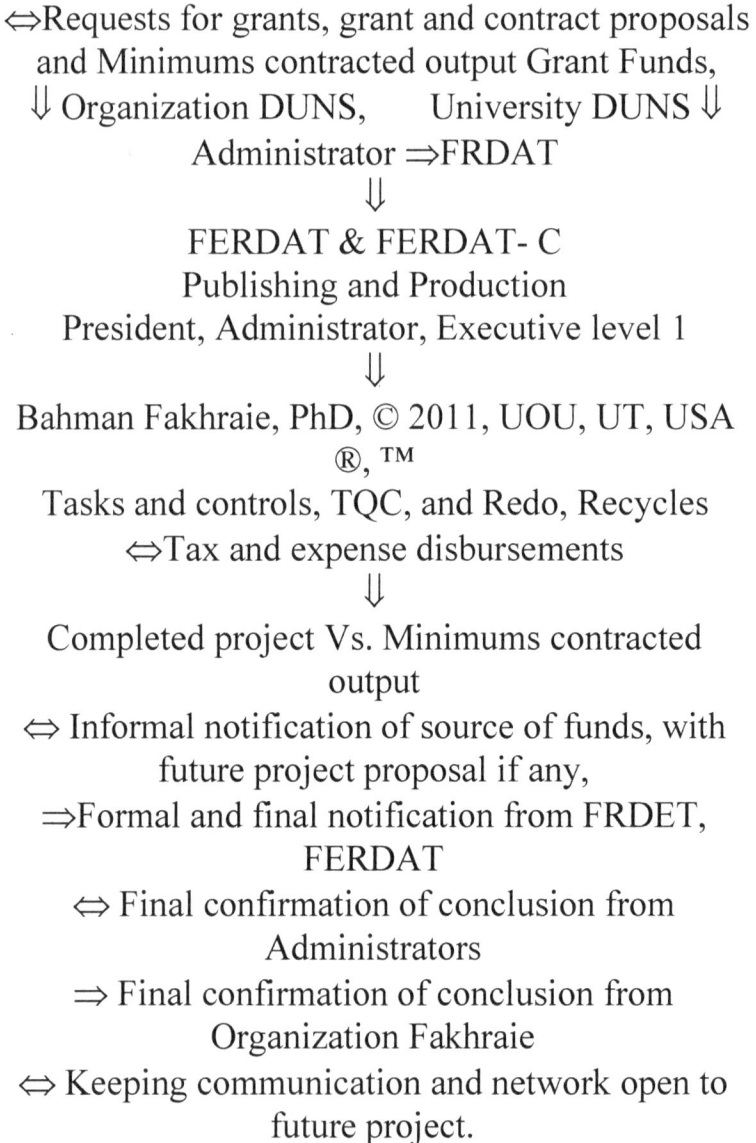

⇔Requests for grants, grant and contract proposals and Minimums contracted output Grant Funds, ⇓ Organization DUNS,   University DUNS ⇓
Administrator ⇒FRDAT
⇓
FERDAT & FERDAT- C
Publishing and Production
President, Administrator, Executive level 1
⇓
Bahman Fakhraie, PhD, © 2011, UOU, UT, USA
®, ™
Tasks and controls, TQC, and Redo, Recycles
⇔Tax and expense disbursements
⇓
Completed project Vs. Minimums contracted output
⇔ Informal notification of source of funds, with future project proposal if any,
⇒Formal and final notification from FRDET, FERDAT
⇔ Final confirmation of conclusion from Administrators
⇒ Final confirmation of conclusion from Organization Fakhraie
⇔ Keeping communication and network open to future project.

Bahman Fakhraie, PhD, © ® ™ 2010-, UOU, UT, USA

Section 6, DATA MANAGEMENT:

Relevant data will be managed, and stored. Moreover, the data and the progression of data used will be stored post completion. As a common practice, Dr. Bahman Fakhraie will, also preserve a historical over view of data for legal purposes, for future use. A portion of that will be shared if requested in written form, post settlement of all expenses. The ethical requirements will be followed in accordance with the applied law established.

The final product will be shared with the grantors, after all the financial settlements have been met. The reviewers will have access to a portion of the progress. All publications or Grant-products are published on completion for academic and educational research, USA Library of Congress, trade journals, FERDAT Publishing, author's websites, other academic journals, etc.

All rights will revert back to author after 3 years, if contract exits for limited rights.

Labor laws and benefit distribution will be according to the institutional Fed Cap limits, private contracts; vendors are responsible for their own legal obligations. (Publication Ink, FedExx, kinkcos, vendors etc.)

CPA and Legal establishment, outside to this entity will be contracted to handle more complex issues when they arise, all cost are due, prior to any such required actions are requested.

Full transparencies are practiced for authorized agents only, mostly through the internet, after proper signatures are obtained. All copyrights and proprietary rights are granted, accorded and reserved to Dr. Bahman Fakhraie,

All future development, educational development will have to be contracted, or signed out temporarily, they will revert to Dr. Bahman Fakhraie, in case of any and all legal issues.

These and other clauses will be amended and upgraded as required over time, they all apply.

Absolut or required non-disclosures by the firm or Dr. Fakhraie will require pre-paid plan with minimum flooring pay. Flex-legalism targeted at the firm, or Dr. B. Fakhraie will be due cause for nonpaid termination by the same.

G. Any and All Risks or Harms invokes these legal clauses. The Following legal clauses are base minimum, and will not limit all rights and legal protection, with uniform constitutional rights they are implied and accorded. Contractually all rights are implied and accorded. Please, read all the legal notes before using any materials.

Sec 7, Check CURRICULUM VITA

CURRICULUM VITA

Bahman Fakhraie, PhD, UOU, UT, USA
University Of Utah, Economic Dept., U. O. U.;   Salt Lake City, Utah USA, 84112
Permanent Address: c/o 1120 Canyon Rd No. 29; Ogden Utah 84404
E-Mail: bf9@utah.edu , bahf.econ@gmail.com, dr.bahf.econ@gmail.com
Dr. Bahman Fakhraie's Books webpage,
http://bahfecon.wix.com/bahfecon

Honors and Awards: **Omicron Delta Epsilon Honor Society**

Utah State U. USA, **Certificates Keys to Agricultural Development at the Local Level**

Student Leadership Positions: **President of International Student Association** [ASUSU]

Bachelor of Science: **Utah State University**

Master of Science: **Utah State University**

PhD, University of Utah   **University of Utah**

PhD, Economics (international economics), University of Utah

Certificate of Completion, PhD in Economics University of Utah, 2010

Certificate of Completion, PhD in Economics University of Chicago, 2011

Mission Statement:

To formulate optimum functionality in management teams, in order to make profitable and beneficial contributions, and create opportunity for merited advancements.

Utilizing rare combination of theory and empiricism, cultivated in multi-cultural inclusive settings in academic and private enterprise, I enhance the productivity and completion of project management. Experiences, among fields of International Trade, Managerial, and Production theories in Economics, Finance, and Business, which modern business and academic institutions find very expensive to employ and too costly not to employ. The extensive background helps advance research in my field of study.

Goals:

I have initiated, passed, and funded many constructive projects --goals by committees--, where it has been value enhancing and mutually beneficial individually, and by team assists. Private Senior Economist: Research Positions with Contracts, Teaching, Research, Books, with contract.

Short Term Private Contracts are for economic and financial educational consultations.

Academic Preparatory Continuum:

PhD, University of Utah, Dissertation:

TECHNOLOGICAL INJECTION, DYNAMIC NEW CAPITAL MEASUREMENTS AND PRODUCTION THEORY IN ECONOMICS

Thesis statement:

The dynamic influences of technology and elemental factors of production --defined and measured in this dissertation-- are greater than commonly have been calculated or expected. The impacts of different measurements of capital stocks (traditional and new adjusted capital) on embodied and disembodied technological variables, on productivity, and economic growth of national social products are tested. The econometric effects of two new capital stock measures introduced in the writing of Friedrich August Von Hayek, John Maynard Keynes, and further developed by Evsey D. Domar, and ignored by most modern economists are examined. Therefore, we focus on the demand and supply side of technological embodied in capital, in human skill and produced goods and services, and the economy. Dr. Bahman Fakhraie's Book-link is at,

Post-Doctoral Research and Goals:

1. Updating the econometrics of the dissertation to most recent available data and dates, (per available grants)

2. Include, countries, with acceptable data in the study, set up formulaic development in excel etc. for use. (per grants)

3. Focus on the theoretical advancement in production processes for systemic innovational additive methodologies, in Movie production, Agriculture, and other creative industries, using existing or newly hired faculties, in anchored and linked institutions. This is a great serious work in shadows of Adam Smith, Schumpeter, Hayak, and Keynes.

    Teconomics: Scientific Synthesis of Economics and Technology in Teconomics

4. Stream line methodologies, and project for PhD Students, master students, and introductory fields' level, an extension of the dissertation and current copyrighted writings.

5. A multimedia production of Dr. Fakhraie's recent research,
NEW DYNAMIC ECONOMIC MODELS TO STUDY TECHNOLOGY INJECTIONS & DYNAMIC CAPITAL FORMATION, IMPACTS ON INTERNATIONAL TRADE, EXCHANGE RATE, AND GLOBAL ECONOMIC OPTIMASATION

    Presentation by Dr. Bahman Fakhraie

6. Of course, this will be under Sec G of private contract and without infringing on rights of marketing, publishing, and distribution of the same. Certain contracts will be more restrictive, including specific names.

7. Finish the books series in post dissertation Teconomic studies, Micro, Macro, Teconometrics, Teconomic Analysis, and Political Teconomics. (in progress)

Books, published: DR. Bahman Fakhraie's Books web page at, http://bahfecon.wix.com/bahfecon

Dr. Bahman Fakhraie, *TECONOMIC OF VERBALISM,* Utah, FERDAT publishing 2012, a

Paperback link is at, https://www.createspace.com/4121720 The EBook Link is at,

http://www.amazon.com/dp/B00B1LO7UQ

Books web page at, http://bahfecon.wix.com/bahfecon

- *Demand and supply Sides of Technological Injections*, Utah, FERDAT Publishing, 2004, And at,
  http://www.amazon.com/dp/098529583X/ref=rdr_ext_tmb reader_098529583X

- *Teconomics: the microeconomic analysis*, Utah, FERDAT publishing 2012, and,
  https://www.createspace.com/4196760, Books web page at,
  http://bahfecon.wix.com/bahfecon

- *Technological injection, dynamic new capital measurements, and Production Theory in Economics*, (Michigan: ProQuest LLC, 2010) and,
  https://order.proquest.com/OA_HTML/pqdtibeCCtpItmDspRte.jsp
  Books web page at,
  http://bahfecon.wix.com/bahfecon

- *Teconomics of Verbalism*, Utah FERDAT Publishing 2012, and at,
  https://www.createspace.com/4121720,
  Books web page at,
  http://bahfecon.wix.com/bahfecon

- *Analytical Remedies for The Millennial Cascading Economic Declines,* Utah FERDAT Publishing 2012, and at, https://www.createspace.com/4187823,
- "The Demand and Supply Sides of Appropriate Technological Advancement." (Research paper at University of Utah Economics Dept. 2003),
- "Economic Theories and Practices in Technological Changes, capital measures, and Production." (Research paper at University of Utah Economics Dept. 1988).
- Fakhraie, Bahman, "The Demand and Supply Sides of Appropriate Technological Advancement." (Research paper at University of Utah Economics Dept. 2003).
- "Hallowing headless nations? The need to invest on public education under the 1980s international economic conditions," (Research paper at University of Utah Economics Dept. 1988).
- "Transfer of Technologies and Socioeconomic Theories of Dualism," (Research paper at University of Utah Economics Dept. 1983).

Production theory in Agriculture
Agro-production, Sheep production in Iran (an onsite research project 1975)
Monetary Macroeconomic Specialization (Milton Freedman,)
International Monetary macroeconomic Specializations (Robert Mundell)
Fiscal Analysis of oscillatory modifications
Applied Agricultural production in developing economies
Inappropriate Technology Transfers by Corporations
and dualistic induced instabilities in a pre-democratic economies.
Certificate in Rural Development from Utah State University
Research Skills:

Statistical packages, data selection, analysis, and formulations.

Computer Languages, Spread Sheet Data Analysis, Writings

Multimedia & Creative Skills: Film and video production, CD: audio and video works

Languages: Fluent in English and Farsi, I can read and write some French, and Arabic.

Fluent in Dezfili Dari dialectic [One of the earliest spoken languages]

Teaching Experiences:

University of Utah: macroeconomic and microeconomic: introductory course, and related mathematics.

Utah State University: Economic Department, Persian language, and cultural studies to faculty and students, and teaching assistance for Agricultural economics.

Volunteer Helping of other students

Student leadership positions AUSU, as an undergraduate

PROFESSIONAL EXPERIENCE:

Founder and Management of Money Wise Firm (A Private Financial Education Foundation for Personal Financial studies), 1970 to date

Volunteer work: President; V.P., and Treasurer of Cherrywood Association Inc., multimillion dollars project, (Different 3 year cycles 1980 to 1999, consultation to date)

Real Estate Investor and Renovations, General Manger, to date

Agribusiness management, owner manager

Auto Agency sale manager/sold

Auto shop management/sold

Numerous Volunteer Projects: planning, budgeting, contracting, and finishing.

Beside educational publications, and digital multi-media CDS, DVD formats, copyrighted at USA the library of congress.

Other Experience:

Budget Analysis, Budget Setting, Budget Forecasting, Asset Allocation Studies, Portfolio Analysis Studies, Saving (Goal Setting) Plan, Tax Management Studies, Risk/Reward Management and studies, Economic Condition risk Analysis, Managerial Goal Setting and Project Production Process and Enactments.

Economic Topics of Research and Lectures:
 Non-Marxist Revolutions in Middle East (Iran)
 Economic and Indices (Measurement Issues)
 Economic Theories of Technological Changes and Capital Measures
 Technological Change, Growth Rate, and Capital Formations with US Data
 Education and Taxation
 Hollowing Headless Nations! Education Crisis
 Technological Parameters Statistical Measurements
 New Econometric Measurements of Capital in Production Theory

Reading (Economic, Science, Mathematics, Econometrics, Statistics, Mystery, Ancients), Films (art, industry), Jazz, Foreign Eclectics music, Fly-fishing

Techonological Injection, Dynamic New Capital measirements, and Production Theory in Economics

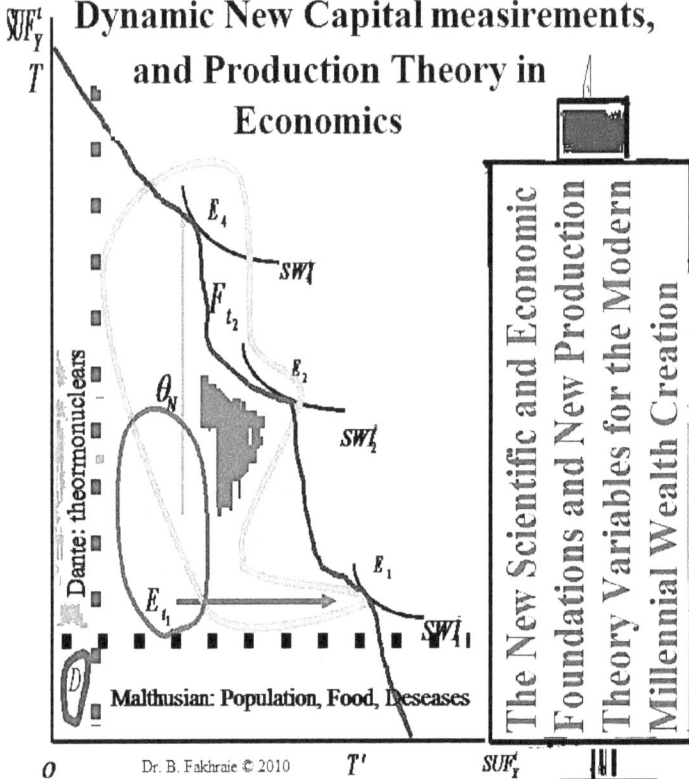

The New Scientific and Economic Foundations and New Production Theory Variables for the Modern Millennial Wealth Creation

Dr. B. Fakhraie © 2010

Supply

Demand

Technological injections

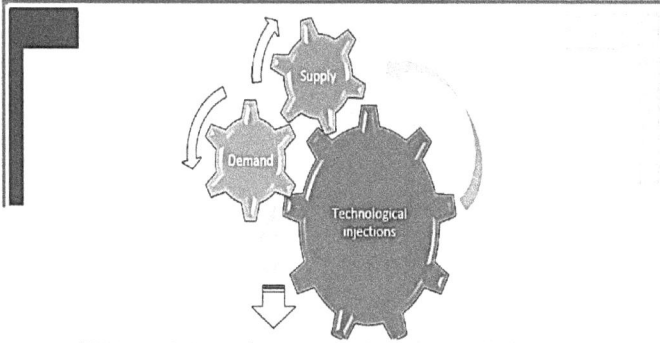

TECONOMIC ANALYSIS
AND REMEDIES FOR
THE MILLENNIALCASCADING
ECONOMIES

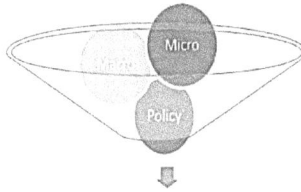

Micro

Policy

Solutions, beside repeating past mistakes.

Dr. Bahman Fakhraie's books,
http://drbahfecon.wix.com/teconomics

Striped Subset: Trade surplus
sustainable optimization possible

Environmental Factors:
1-Lethaly toxic
2-Non-toxic

Doted Subset:
Profit maximization
porbabale

TECONOMICS

Economics:
1-Relative competetion
2-Non competetive

Political Conditions:
1-Relative democracy
2-Non-demcratic

SCIENTIFIC SYNTHESIS OF MICROECONOMICS
AND TECHNOLOGICAL INJECTIONS
IN ECONOMICS

Global Trade:
1-Free trade
2-Limted trade

Dr. Bahman Fakhraie © 2010

THE MILLENNIAL POLITICAL ECONOMIC PARADIGM

Dr. Bahman Fakhraie's books,
http://bahfecon.wix.com/bahfecon

TREATISE ON
TECONOMICS
ØF
DYNAMIC RISKS

ALL NATURAL DISASTERS,

&

Energy Resources Production Disasters

Bahman Fakhraie, Ph.D.

Dr. Bahman Fakhraie *Teconomics of Dynamic Risks*

TECONOMICS

ØF

CATASTROPHES

ALL NATURAL DISASTERS

DYNAMIC RISKS

&

Energy Resources Production Disasters

Bahman Fakhraie, Ph.D.

Teconomics Of USA Elections and Extremisms

Author, Dr. Bahman Fakhraie
Copyright Case No. 1-2766536451
ISBN-10:0996633499
ISBN-13:978-0-9966334-9-9

www.ingramcontent.com/pod-product-compliance
Lightning Source LLC
Chambersburg PA
CBHW050719280326
41926CB00088B/3308